Puppets

Helen and Peter McNiven

LSCA student non-fiction grant

With photographs by Chris Fairclough

Thomson Learning • New York

FIRST ARTS & CRAFTS

Books in this series

Collage
Drawing
Making Masks
Models
Painting
Printing
Puppets
Toys and Games

For Jack

First published in the
United States in 1995 by
Thomson Learning
115 Fifth Avenue
New York, NY 10003

First published in Great Britain in 1994 by Wayland (Publishers) Ltd.

Library of Congress Cataloging-in-Publication Data
McNiven, Helen and Peter.
  Puppets/Helen and Peter McNiven; with photographs by Chris Fairclough.
      p.   cm.—(First arts & crafts)
  Includes bibliographical references and index.
  ISBN 1-56847-215-3
  1. Puppet making—Juvenile literature. [1. Puppet making.
2. Handicraft.] I. McNiven, Peter (Peter Alister) II. Fairclough,
Chris, ill. III. Title. IV. Series.
TT174.7.M36   1994
745.592'24—dc20   94-26043

Printed in Italy

Contents

What are puppets?

The first puppets were made a very long time ago. Ancient peoples used puppets to act out stories and to please their gods. Each puppet would be made for the special part it would play.

Way-Yang Indonesian rod puppet.

Today you can see puppets at festivals and on television.

Puppet theaters still travel around the world telling stories that are hundreds of years old.

There are four main types of puppet:

A **hand puppet** is worn on the hand, like a glove. When the hand and fingers move, the puppet moves.

Shadow puppets are simple flat shapes that are sometimes brightly colored. When they are held between an old sheet and a bright light, the puppets' shadows appear on the sheet.

A **rod puppet** has sticks attached to its hands and

head. Moving the sticks makes the puppet move.

A **string puppet** is also called a marionette. It hangs on strings that are pulled to make the puppet do things like walk or dance.

Puppets can be made out of almost anything. Most of the puppets in this book can be made with a few simple art supplies and other household items.

Always ask an adult for help when cutting things or doing something that might be difficult. Always read all the directions before you start a project.

Rod puppet

String puppet

Hand puppet

Shadow puppet

Once you've made a puppet, you can bring it to life by moving it and being its voice. Make more than one puppet and put on a show with your friends.

5

Finger farm

Finger puppets are easy to make with papier-mâché. The papier-mâché can be built into lots of interesting shapes. Once the puppets are made, put them on your fingers and wiggle them around.

You will need:
Old newspapers
Water
White glue
A bucket or large bowl
Clear tape
Water-based paints

First, make some papier-mâché. Ask an adult to help you.

- Tear some newspaper into small pieces.
- Put the pieces of newspaper in a bucket or large bowl and cover them with warm water.
- Let stand for a few hours until the newspaper is soaking wet. Pour the water off the newspaper.
- With your hands, mix enough white glue into the newspaper to make it soft and sticky.

Now you can make your puppets.

- Wrap a piece of dry newspaper around and around your biggest finger. Use some clear tape to hold it in place.
- Press papier-mâché thickly around the paper on your finger.
- When the paper around your finger is completely covered, carefully slide the shape off and put it to the side to dry.
- Make four or five shapes like this.
- Now add eyes, noses, and ears with more papier-mâché. You could shape your puppets into farm animals. Let them dry for at least two days and then paint them.

Next time, try making a family or zoo animals.

A troupe of dancers

Look at pictures of people dancing, especially at festivals. What sort of dances do they do? What clothes or costumes do they wear? Many peoples across the world dance with puppets to celebrate things such as the seasons.

You will need:

Cardboard

Pencil

Ruler

Scissors

Crayons or paints

Magazines

These dancing puppets also use your fingers, but this time your fingers become the puppets' legs.

What sort of dancers can you make? Collect some pictures from old magazines for ideas.

- Draw your dancers on cardboard. Make them 4 inches high by 2½ inches wide. Don't add the legs, but draw down to an inch below the waist.
- Cut out each dancer. Then cut two holes about half an inch across and a quarter inch apart for your fingers.
- Color your dancers.

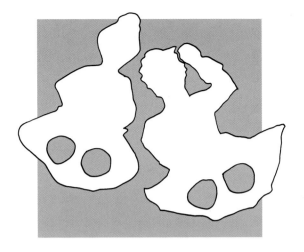

Push two fingers through the holes in the bottom of a puppet. Put on some music and let your fingers dance.

Make shoes from pen caps or paint your fingernails. Wear gloves to give your dancer tights. Glue pieces of fabric or yarn and feathers or beads onto the puppets to make them more exciting.

Mops and brushes

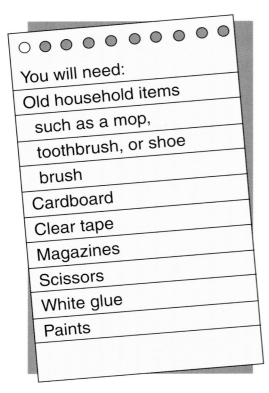
Household objects can make very funny puppets. Ask an adult if there are some old mops or brushes you can use.

Hold a floor mop just below where it joins the handle. The mop becomes a puppet's head of hair.

Make sure the mops and brushes are clean.

Look at this sculpture. It is called an "objet trouvé," which is French for "found object."

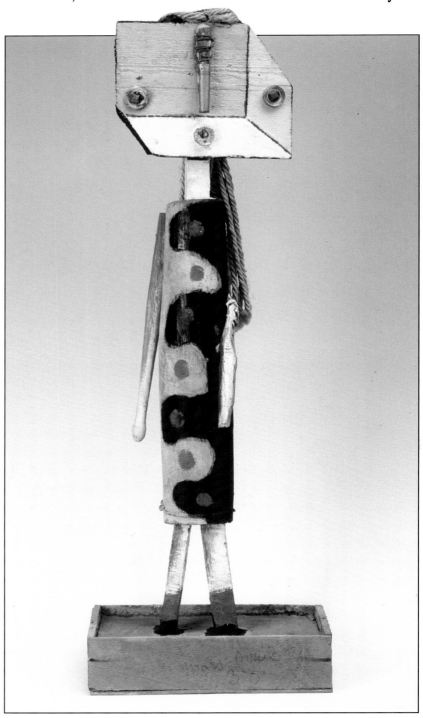

Figure 1935 by Pablo Picasso (1881-1973). Painted wood, string, and wire, with a clay and wood base. Private collection.

- Paint eyes on cardboard or find pictures of eyes in a magazine. Glue or tape them onto the mop head, or use sunglasses.

You can glue or tape on a mouth. Draw one or cut one out of a magazine. Push a finger through the mop for a nose.

You could make a caterpillar from an old shoe brush.

- Paint the wooden part of the brush with green and yellow stripes.
- When the paint is dry, add some eyes.

Make a saucepan lid into a face with the handle as its nose. Use tape to attach the rest of the face so it can be removed easily. What other puppets can you think of to make?

Punch and Judy

Mr. Punch and his wife Judy are puppet characters who have been around for hundreds of years. Find out about the story of Punch and Judy. Who are the other people and animals in the story?

Mr. Punch is very moody. Sometimes he is happy and sometimes he is angry. He makes everyone else happy or angry, too.

You can make your own Punch and Judy puppets.

You will need:

Cardboard

Pencil

Crayons or paints

White glue

Scissors

Thin sticks (like the green sticks used in gardens)

- Fold a piece of cardboard in half with the fold at the bottom. Draw a big and happy Mr. Punch on one side of the cardboard.
- Cut out Mr. Punch through both thicknesses. This will give you two Mr. Punch shapes that are the same. Be careful – don't cut away the fold.
- Turn the cardboard over. Now draw Mr. Punch on the blank side. This time make him look angry.
- Brightly color or paint your Mr. Punch shapes. Cut a small slot in the fold and slide in a stick.
- Glue the shapes together with the stick handle in the middle.

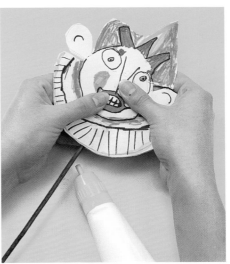

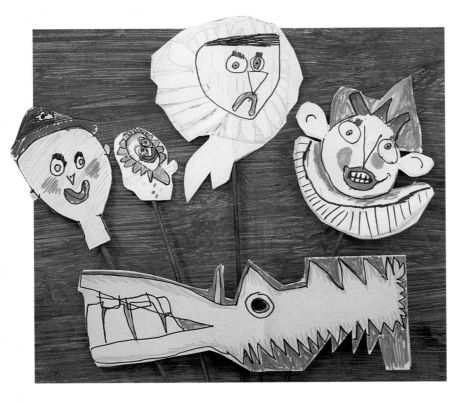

Make Judy, a policeman, a baby, and a crocodile in the same way.

Now you can put on your own Punch and Judy show. Practice with silly voices and sound effects.

13

Swimming fish

Look at lots of pictures of fish. Look at their shapes, colors, and patterns. Other things live underwater, too, like seaweed and crabs. You can make an underwater scene with fish that seem to swim.

You will need:
Cardboard
Crayons or paints
Pencil
Scissors
Paper fasteners or string
Glue
Thin garden sticks
Paints
Colored foil, sequins
Straw and cup of water
Tissue paper

- Draw a big, long fish shape onto a piece of cardboard. Color it with crayons or paints.
- Cut out your fish, then cut it into three pieces – head, body, and tail.
- Fit the pieces back together so that they overlap. Make a hole through each overlap and join with a paper fastener or knotted string.
- Glue the top of a stick to the head and another to the tail of your fish. These rods will make your fish move.

Make more fish with different shapes and patterns for your underwater theater. Stick colored foil, sequins, and other things onto your fish to make them more colorful.

You can make gurgling sounds by blowing bubbles through a straw in a cup of water. You can use torn tissue paper for seaweed.

You can also use your fish as shadow puppets.

- Sit behind a pinned-up sheet with your family or friends on the other side. Turn on a light behind your puppets.
- Hold your puppets up near the sheet and make them swim around. Your audience will be able to see the moving shadows of your puppets.

15

Witch on a stick

Look at this amazing painting of witches.

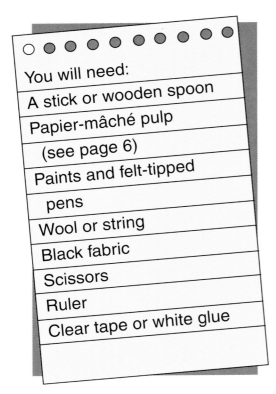

You will need:

A stick or wooden spoon

Papier-mâché pulp
  (see page 6)

Paints and felt-tipped
  pens

Wool or string

Black fabric

Scissors

Ruler

Clear tape or white glue

Part of *The Spell* 1797 by Francisco de Goya (1746-1828).

Witches, elves, and goblins are always scary fun. Think of all the stories you know with bad witches and nasty goblins, and then make yourself a really ugly witch puppet.

- Make the witch's head by pressing papier mâché around the end of a stick or wooden spoon. Build it into a long egg shape.
- Make a big nose with a wart and a long, pointed chin. With your finger, push in holes for eyes.
- Let the head dry for at least two days.

Now paint it weird and wonderful colors. Paint the skin, then eyes and a mouth. Glue on string or yarn for the hair.

Now make the clothing. Ask an adult to help you cut it out.

- Cut out a circle of black fabric, about 12 inches across.
- Cut a hole about half an inch wide in the middle of the circle.
- Turn your witch upside down and push the bottom of the stick or spoon through the hole in the fabric. Push the fabric down to the witch's head.
- Glue or tightly tape the fabric to the stick.

Turn your puppet the right way up. Now your ugly witch is ready for trouble.

You can make all sorts of horrible characters like this to frighten your friends.

17

Indonesian dancer

Rod puppets are very popular in countries like Indonesia where dancers mostly move only their heads and hands to the music. Your puppet could look like this one, or like your favorite star.

You will need:

A small balloon, newspapers, and paste of flour, white glue, and warm water

Papier-mâché pulp (page 6)

Paints

Yarn

Scissors

Ruler

3 thin garden sticks

Clear tape, Glue

Knitting needle

Cardboard

String (2 feet long)

Fabric scraps

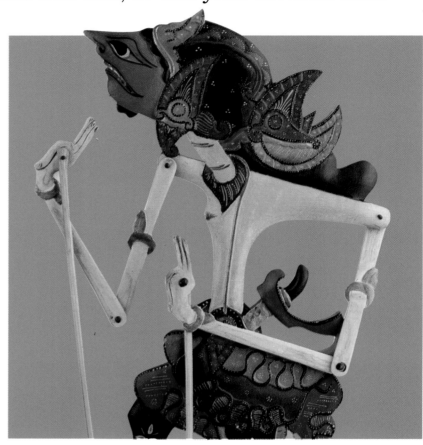

Wangapati puppet from Indonesia.

- Blow up the balloon to the size of a tennis ball.
- Cover the balloon with pieces of torn newspaper dipped in the flour, white glue, and water paste. Put on four layers of newspaper. Let it dry for at least two days and then pop the balloon.

This is your puppet's head. Build up the nose, eyebrows, and chin with papier-mâché pulp. Let it dry. Paint it and glue on yarn for hair. Push a stick into the hole at the base and attach with tape.

Now make moving arms for your puppet.

- On one end of two sticks, model a hand out of papier-mâché. Make a small hole in each wrist with a knitting needle. Paint the hands when they are dry.
- Roll up two pieces of thin cardboard, 6 inches long and 3 inches wide, to make two tubes about half an inch across. Cut each tube in half and wrap clear tape around each half to keep it rolled up.

Now you can put the puppet together.

- Wind the middle of the string around the puppet's neck twice, 2 inches below the head. Hold it in place with clear tape.
- Push one end of the string through two tubes, then glue it into the hole in one of the hands.
- Do the same with the other tubes and hand.
- Dress your dancer with fabric scraps.

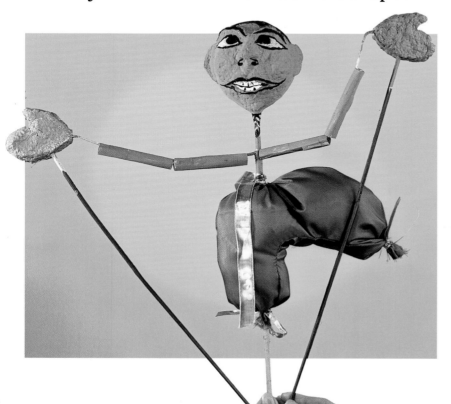

Hold one of the "arm" sticks in one hand and the other two sticks in the other hand. Practice moving your puppet. Now you are ready to make your puppet dance.

These make very good shadow puppets, too.

Quick change

These hand puppets have brightly colored costumes. Hand puppets are sometimes called glove puppets because they are worn like gloves.

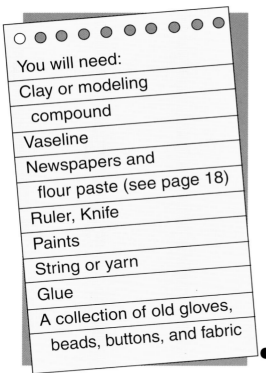

You will need:

Clay or modeling compound

Vaseline

Newspapers and flour paste (see page 18)

Ruler, Knife

Paints

String or yarn

Glue

A collection of old gloves, beads, buttons, and fabric

Your puppet will be made from a glove. You can make as many different gloves as you like. The puppet's head is not joined to the glove, so your puppet can change costumes very quickly!

Start by making the head from clay or modeling compound.

● Roll a ball shape slightly smaller than a tennis ball. This is the head.
● To make the neck, make another ball and roll it into a sausage between your hands and then on a work top. Coil this to form a circle about 3 inches across. Press the head onto the neck and smooth them together.

Now use your fingers to model the shapes of a face – nose, lips, eyes. To help you, look at pictures of people, or look in a mirror at the shapes of your own face. Don't forget to add the ears.

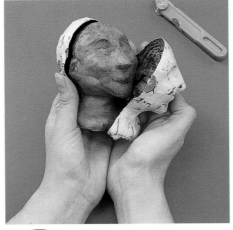

- Cover the head with Vaseline and layer it with newspaper and flour paste. Let it dry for at least two days.
- Ask an adult to cut around the head, over the top, through the dry layers of newspaper, with a knife. Carefully pull the papier-mâché halves away.
- Stick them back together with more paste and strips of newspaper.

Let the head dry, then paint it and glue on string or yarn for hair. Put a glove on your hand and place your puppet's head over the middle three fingers.

Decorate your gloves with buttons, beads, and pieces of fabric to make different costumes.

A mole in the garden

You can make a very simple puppet out of a sock worn over your hand and arm. How about a mole?

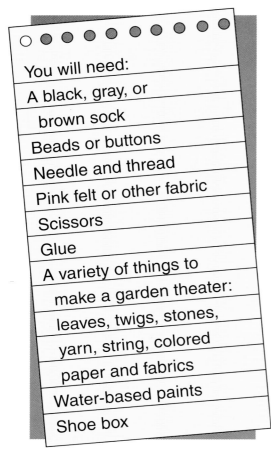

You will need:

A black, gray, or brown sock

Beads or buttons

Needle and thread

Pink felt or other fabric

Scissors

Glue

A variety of things to make a garden theater: leaves, twigs, stones, yarn, string, colored paper and fabrics

Water-based paints

Shoe box

Your sock puppet will have its own theater.

- On your sock, glue or sew a button or bead onto the area of the middle toe. This is your mole's nose.
- Cut out four feet from pink felt or another fabric. Glue these onto the sock.

Now make your mole's garden. You will need leaves, twigs, and stones from your yard or a park. You can also use other things like yarn, string, fabric, or crumpled, colored paper to build your garden theater.

- In one end of your shoe box, cut a hole big enough for your hand and arm to push through. This is the entrance for your mole puppet.
- Cut smaller holes in one of the sides. These are for your fingers to play wriggling worms.

Now build your garden scene in and around the shoe box using the different things you have collected.

Push your mole puppet through the big hole. Now push your painted fingers through the small holes. Move your puppets around and you have a mole and some worms under the ground.

The ugly duckling

A string puppet can walk with you anywhere. You will need some help with this ugly duckling. Make sure you look closely at the pictures, and read all the directions before you start. Once you've got the idea, you can make other string puppets.

You will need:

2 toilet paper tubes

Ruler

Scissors

Cardboard

Pencil

Large needle

Clear tape

2 dowel rods

String

Two small coins

Glue

Paints, feathers, colored paper

- Cut a small quarter-inch "V" in each end of one toilet paper tube.
- From one end of the tube, cut a 3-inch slit down two sides.
- Draw a bird's wings and tail on cardboard, like the ones shown below. Cut them out and slide them into the slits in your tube.
- Cut a head from the other tube. Make a hole through it from top to bottom with a large needle.
- Cut out a half-circle of cardboard (the flat side of the half-circle should be the length of your tube). Use clear tape to attach this to the bottom of your tube to look like a bird's belly.
- Cut out two feet from cardboard.

Tape the two dowel rods together in the shape of a cross.

Cut a piece of string 27 inches long.

- Hang the tube in the middle of the string. Tie a knot in one end of the string about an inch above the tube. Thread the head onto this string. Tie each end of the string to each end of one of the dowels.

Cut two more pieces of string, each about 20 inches long.

- Make a knot in one end of one piece. Slide this to the end of one of the slits in the tube so that the knot is inside the bird's body. Thread a foot onto the string about 4 inches from the tube.
- Do the same with the other piece of string.
- Tie the strings to each end of the second dowel. Make sure they are the same length.

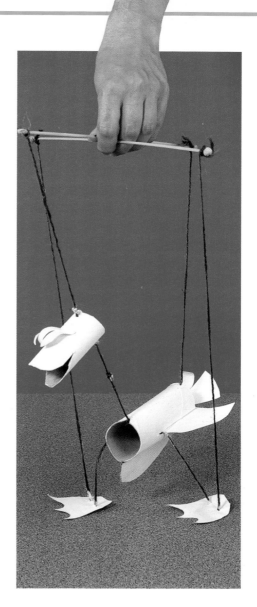

Glue coins to the bottoms of the feet to make the legs hang down. Now you have a duckling you can take for a walk. Decorate it with paints, feathers, and paper curls.

I am a robot

This is a robot. It is a machine that will obey your orders.

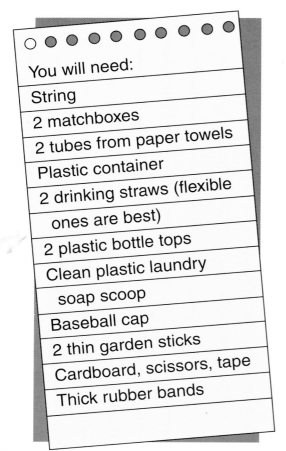

You will need:

String

2 matchboxes

2 tubes from paper towels

Plastic container

2 drinking straws (flexible ones are best)

2 plastic bottle tops

Clean plastic laundry soap scoop

Baseball cap

2 thin garden sticks

Cardboard, scissors, tape

Thick rubber bands

You can make a very smart puppet. It will do what you do. Use lots of different things to make it. Ask an adult to help you make the holes for the string. Look at the pictures carefully to see how the puppet is put together.

- Cut 3 feet of string and knot one end.
- Push the other end through holes in the end of one matchbox, then through one tube, the plastic container, and back down through the second tube and matchbox. Pull the string tight and tie a knot.

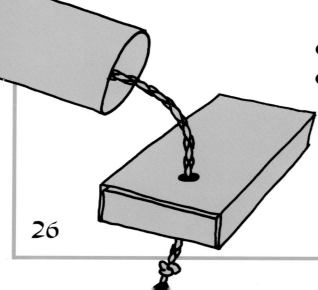

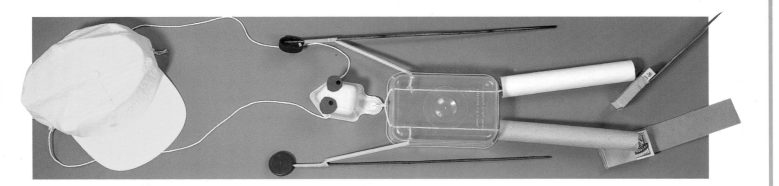

- Cut 16 inches of string and knot one end.
- Push the other end through a bottle top, a straw, then through the top of the plastic container. Pull the string tight and make a knot. Repeat on the other side.
- Tie the laundry soap scoop to the top of the container.
- Cut two pieces of stiff cardboard 10 inches by 1½ inches. Glue them firmly to the bottom of the matchboxes.

To make your robot work:

- Join your robot's head to a baseball cap with two strings.
- Make a hole in the back of each straw near the hands. Slide in garden sticks.
- Stand on the cardboard at the back of the matchboxes. Ask an adult to attach the puppet to your feet with rubber bands. Put the cap on your head, move your hands and feet, and your robot will follow!

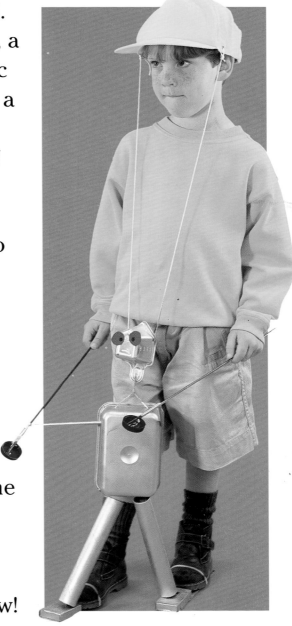

Puppet theaters

Don't keep your puppets to yourself. Get together with some friends and put on a show.

There are lots of different ways to make a theater for your puppets. Some are temporary and quick to put up, and others can be used again and again.

Place two chairs about 3 feet apart and rest a broom across the tops. Hang an old sheet or blanket over the broom. Hide behind the sheet and make your puppets play above it.

You can make a very simple theater in a doorway. Ask an adult to help you hang a piece of fabric or an old towel across the bottom half of a doorway. Kneel down behind the screen and move your puppets above it.

Add scenery by painting a large piece of paper and hanging it across the top half of the other side of the doorway.

For string puppets, hang the scenery across the bottom half of a doorway on one side and the fabric or towel above it on the other side. Then hang your puppets down in between.

This theater uses big cardboard boxes. Put one box on top of another. Cut out a rectangle in the top box. The bottom box will hide you from your audience. Paint your theater with bright bold patterns. Make a curtain across the front of your theater with some string and a piece of fabric. Make scenery from more cardboard and slide it in.

Helpful hints

You don't need a lot of fancy materials to make a puppet – you need a great imagination and a willingness to experiment, or try new things. What counts as much as how the puppet looks is how you move it and make it speak. Your puppet could be a simple sock, but if it moves in a convincing way or tells an interesting story, it will be a success.

Here are some helpful hints:

- Look at puppets in toy stores and characters in books to get ideas for making your own puppets.

- Ask a friend to make puppets with you.

- Put on a puppet show for your friends. Write a script from your favorite story, or make up your own story. Bang on pots and pans, hit the floor with a shoe, or play a musical instrument to make sound effects. You can even use a tape recorder to record some sound effects, such as a doorbell or telephone ringing, and then play them back for your show.

- Practice your show in front of a mirror so you can see how your puppet moves. Try to make it move as smoothly as possible.

- Keep your puppets in a place where you can admire them when you aren't using them. Hang your string puppets from a bulletin board or a coat hook so they don't get tangled.

Glossary

Act Pretend to be someone or something else.

Audience In this book, the people who watch and listen to a puppet show.

Festivals Large celebrations that can last for days.

Overlap Laying part of one thing over part of another.

Paper fasteners Pins with two long ends. When the pin is pushed through something, such as holes in paper, the two ends are bent back to hold the pin in place.

Scenery The painted pictures that are put behind puppets or actors in a theater to show where the story is taking place: in a room or in a street, for example.

Sculpture A three-dimensional work of art made from solid materials such as wood, metal, or stone. You can usually walk around a sculpture to see it from every side.

Theater The place where people (or puppets) act out plays or stories in front of an audience.

Troupe A group of dancers or actors, especially those who travel together.

Further information

Further reading

Bailey, Vanessa. *Puppets: Games and Projects*. Rainy Days. New York: Gloucester Press, 1991.

Buchwald, Claire: *The Puppet Book: How to Make and Operate Puppets and Stage a Puppet-Play*. Boston: Plays, Inc., 1990.

Philpott, V. and McNeil, M. J. *Puppets: A Simple Guide to Making and Working Puppets*. Tulsa, OK: EDC Publishing, 1977.

Pryor, Nick. *Putting on a Play*. New York: Thomson Learning, 1994.

Supraner, Robyn and Supraner, Lauren. *Plenty of Puppets to Make*. Clever Crafts. Mahwah, NJ: Troll Associates, 1981.

Wright, Lyndie. *Puppets*. Fresh Start. New York: Franklin Watts, 1989.

Index

Acknowledgments

The publishers wish to thank the following for their kind assistance with this book:
The Little Angel Marionette Theatre, London, for puppets on pages 4, 5, 20, and 22, and the marionette on the front cover.
John Styles for all the puppets on p. 12 and the puppet theater on p. 29.

The publishers wish to thank the following for the use of photographs:
Robert Harding Picture Library for p. 8 Ngara Zulu dancing teams © G. M. Wilkins.
The Tate Gallery, London, for p. 10 *Figure* 1935 by Pablo Picasso, Private Collection © DACS 1994.
Oxford Scientific Films Ltd. © Max Gibbs p. 14.
Museo Lazaro Galdiano and The Royal Academy of Arts, London, for p. 16 *The Spell* 1797 by Francisco Goya.
Reproduced by kind permission of Oxfam, p. 18 Wangapati Indonesian rod puppet.
All other photographs © Chris Fairclough Colour Library.

The publishers also wish to thank our models Katie, Jeremy, and Jack, and our young artists Harry, Sophie, and Jack.